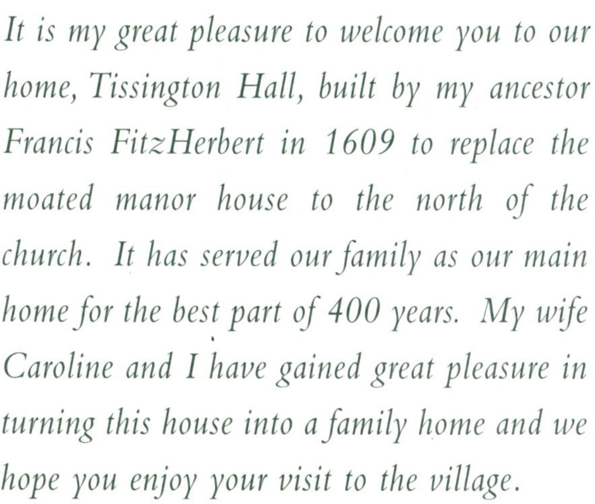

It is my great pleasure to welcome you to our home, Tissington Hall, built by my ancestor Francis FitzHerbert in 1609 to replace the moated manor house to the north of the church. It has served our family as our main home for the best part of 400 years. My wife Caroline and I have gained great pleasure in turning this house into a family home and we hope you enjoy your visit to the village.

Richard FitzHerbert

on the Main Hall
window seat, William
FitzHerbert's grooming kit *c.* 1900
is displayed, next to carved stone rams' heads.

Contents

The FitzHerberts of Tissington

The Estate came into the hands of the FitzHerbert family as the result of Nicholas FitzHerbert marrying the heiress Cicely Francis in the late 15th century.

My family originally came to England with William the Conqueror and settled in Derbyshire when William FitzHerbert was granted the Manor of Norbury in 1125. Subsequent branches were also based at Somersal Herbert. Now the head of the Roman Catholic side of the family - those with a small 'h' - live in Staffordshire at Swynnerton. Our name is spelt with a capital 'H', i.e. FitzHerbert, so that the two branches of the family would be distinguished, although sharing the same surname.

The baronetcy was conferred on William FitzHerbert by George III in 1784 for acting as Minister for Woods and Rivers and for his role as a Gentleman Usher to the King.

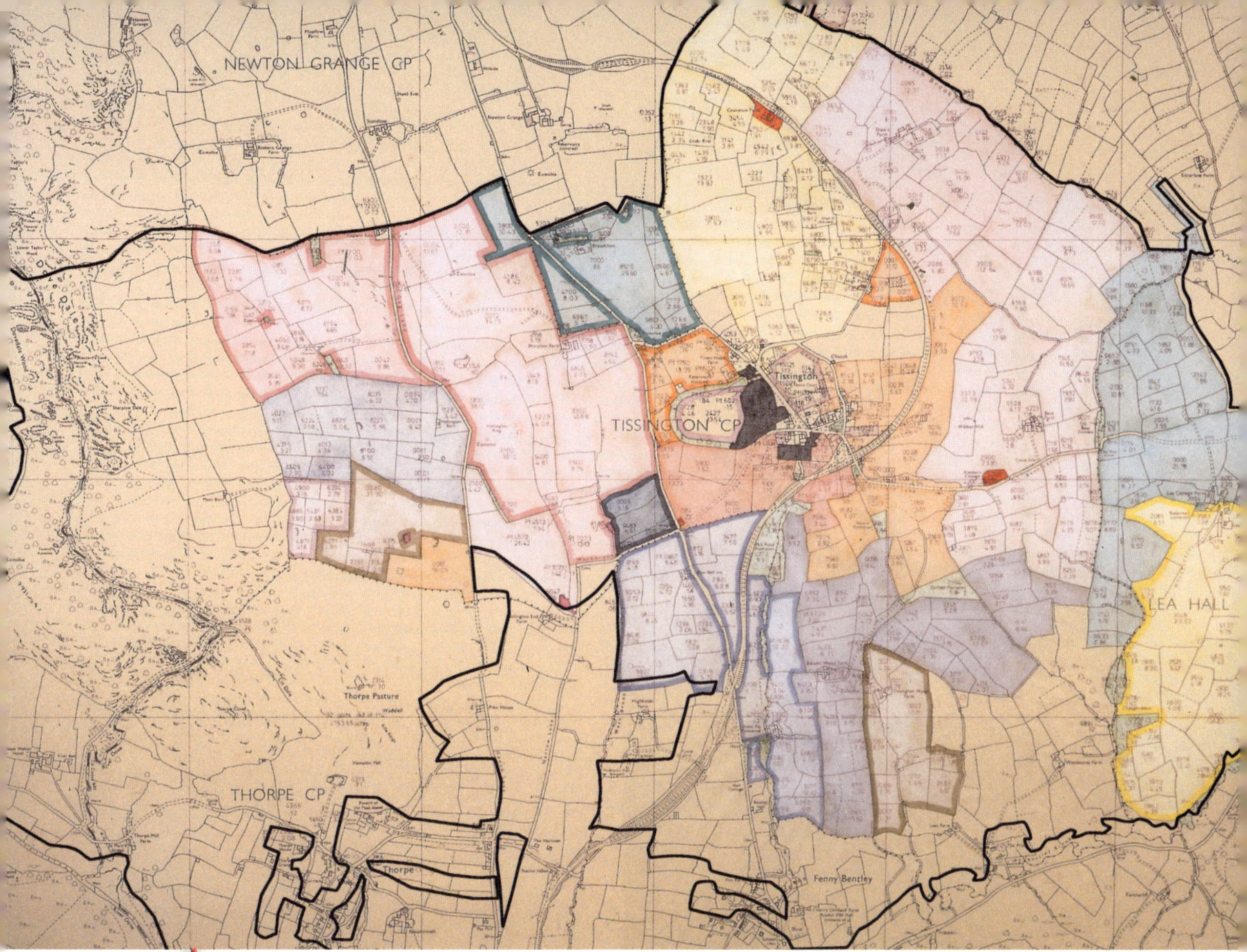

The black outline indicates the size of the Estate in 1938 before its shrinkage, compared to its present size today, as indicated by the coloured areas

He divided his time between London and Derbyshire and was succeeded by his eldest son, Anthony, in 1791. His brother Henry inherited as a minor in 1798 and built extensively in and around the village during his 60 year tenure. Successive baronets have tended diligently to the estate and village although the total acreage has shrunk from about 4,000 acres at its peak in 1850, to 2,400 acres today. The sales were mainly enforced by twentieth century death duties and the cost of Sir Hugo's divorce in 1922.

King George III's seal on the British Ambassador's credentials presented to Catherine the Great by Alleyne FitzHerbert, later Lord St. Helens.

The Lady FitzHerbert

Beginning with her Maiden Voyage in 1829, ***The Lady FitzHerbert*** sailed between the West Indies and London for approximately ten years with cargoes of sugar, rum and coffee, together with some Madeira wine, ginger and pimento. On the outward voyages she was largely in ballast with whatever general cargo could be found, and occasionally, she carried passengers such as on her 3rd voyage in 1830, when passage was provided to 32 troops at 28/6d (£1.50) a day each, plus victualling at the rate of one shilling a day per man for the 90-day voyage.

Sir Henry FitzHerbert also owned *'an extra boat, 'Selina', a deck'd sloop, of adequate capacity to remain in Jamaica for the exclusive use of the ship'.*

Captain Ferrier stayed at Tissington Hall between the 14th-17th October 1835.

The Lady FitzHerbert

386 tons

length 100ft

beam 30ft

draft 13ft

Commander Captain James Ferrier

Crew: Mate, 2nd Mate, Carpenter, Carpenter's Mate, Boatswain, Steward, Cook and 16 Seamen

Front elevation of the Hall from the book of the proposed extensions for Tissington Hall by Jeffrey Wyatville, 1843

Tissington Hall is a house of many extensions; originally built in the early 17th century, a top floor was added around 1700 and then the well-known Derby architect Joseph Pickford remodelled the west aspect around 1780 by adding a projecting central bay and open arcading on the ground floor. The major extension of the Library and Billiard Room wing was completed by the architect Arnold Mitchell for the 5th Baronet, Rev. Sir Richard FitzHerbert in 1902. The other part of Mitchell's brief was to join up the Servants' House to the main Hall. The Staff Wing as it became known, was converted into two separate flats in 1994.

Tissington Village during the 18th century by George Barrett R.A. (1728 - 1784)

The Main Hall

The stone-flagged floor is contemporary with the building of the house in 1609. One of the main features of the room is the stunning ***Gothic fireplace,*** for which I have the original receipt. It reads: *'June 17th, 1757, chimneypiece in hall at Tissington measured and valued by Daniel Hopton and Henry Watson'.* The total value was £54.2s.5½d. Everything is itemised on the bill including the finials, the Gothic head in the centre and a carriage charge termed as *'Carriage and boxes as by Mr. Hall's bill of £3.12s.0d.'*

Other items of interest in the Main Hall are a delightful pair of ***late 18th century bookcases*** by Chippendale and a recently acquired ***rosewood piano*** by Broadwood & Sons - donated to us by some kind friends.

CHIPPENDALE BOOKCASE

A carver from the set of dining-chairs made by Chippendale for the family

Mary Cromwell

Opposite (clockwise from top left): Marble bust of Lord St. Helens by the Dutch sculptor, Nollekens

carved limestone Gargoyle's head *c.* 1757 on the fireplace

Group of water nymphs in marble, late 19th century

bronze head of Hercules

Opposite the fireplace is the ***marble bust of Lord St. Helens*** by the Dutch sculptor, Nollekens. The cap is a new addition. Whilst St. Helens was ambassador and plenipotentiary in Russia, Spain, France and other European countries in the late 18th and early 19th centuries he collected many of the fine things which you will see in the house today.

Jacobean oak armchair 1615

*In keeping with the rest of the house, the room is **panelled in oak,** some of which dates from the 17th century. There are also wonderful Gothic arches and pediments adorning the wall.*

Close up detail of artichokes, from the painting "The Gamedealer"

The Dining Room

In contrast to the Entrance Hall the panelling here is much more regular in style, rather austere, darker and typically Victorian.

This carved oak settle by Garry Passam was commissioned by us to commemorate the Millennium (MM) at Tissington, and the arches bear our initials CLF (Caroline Louise FitzHerbert) and RRF (Richard Ranulph FitzHerbert). It is an exact copy of the late 17th century oak settle already in the Dining Room.

We commissioned the plaque bearing the Family's Coat of Arms. Other examples of Garry's work are at the adjacent Tissington Pre-Prep School.

This walking stick once belonged to William FitzHerbert, 1st baronet (opposite). It was presented to him by King George III, as a gift to commemorate the 1st Baronetcy. The silver top bears the King's royal cypher.

Lord St.Helens
(brother of 1st Baronet)

It is important to keep the curtains shut constantly to prevent the wood panelling from fading. This room was originally the old kitchen before the extensions by Arnold Mitchell in 1900-02. The kitchen range was situated where the small fireplace is today, interestingly small for such a large house.

The table is Regency mahogany by Gillow of Lancaster, with a matching set of thirteen chairs. In addition we are fortunate to have 23 Chippendale chairs, the four carvers having our coat of arms carved on them; three lions on a scarlet background. The ceiling work is by Bankart, added in the early 1900s along with the Library wing. Whether lunchtime or evening, 24 people can enjoy a delightful meal in this charming room, all overseen by my ancestors, staring down from their portraits.

Arrabella Alleyne
by Michael Dahl
(1660 - 1750)

William FitzHerbert
1st Baronet, by Batoni

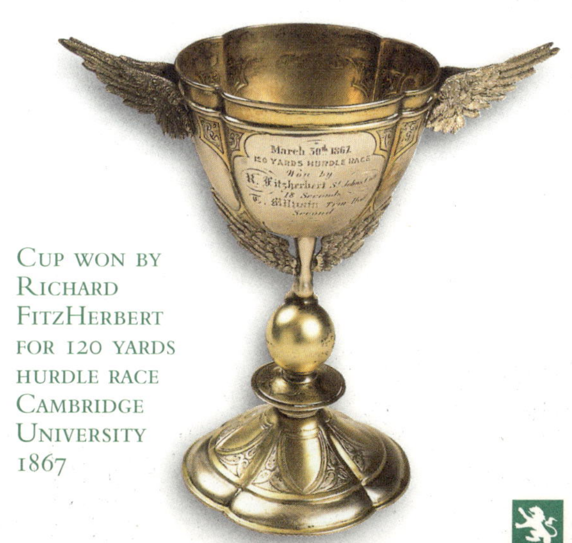

Cup won by
Richard
FitzHerbert
for 120 yards
hurdle race
Cambridge
University
1867

7
8
SCRIPTORES DECEM ANGLICANI
TWYSDEN

THE LIBRARY

This library holds 3,016 books. There are encyclopaedias, a set of Waverley novels, old Spectator omnibus albums and 17th, 18th and 19th century volumes, many of them having the bookplates of Lord St. Helens and Sir Henry and Sir William, the 3rd and 4th Baronets. Although it appears older - probably from the impression of all the old volumes - the room is Mitchell again, created in the early 1900s.

Woodland Frieze by Bankart for Mitchell

below: The Butler's Mirror

Above the fireplace at the west end of the room, is the ***'Butler's Mirror',*** and further up, the most wonderful ***frieze.*** Depicting a woodland scene of trees, birds, flowers, it was created by Bankart for Mitchell, who was passionate about this form of decoration. It would have been rather romantic if it portrayed Tissington, but it could be of any country estate.

You can also see the splendid bracket clock made by Jasper Taylor of Holborn in about 1907. It was presented to the Honourable Margaret Eleanor Holmes à Court, who was my grandmother, by the inhabitants of the villages of Heytesbury, Titherington and Knock, on her marriage to my grandfather Henry Edward FitzHerbert on April 4th 1907. The clock is still one of the best timekeepers in the room - with the most wonderful tick.

Tapestry cushion of Tissington Hall by Selina FitzHerbert, 2003 (it took six years to complete)

7
19 70
BURKE'S
PEERAGE
BARONETAGE
&
KNIGHTAGE
105TH EDITION
BURKE'S PEERAGE LT
8

The Stairway

INLAY DETAIL OF CARVED OAK SERPENT AT THE BASE OF THE STAIRS

The highly impressive Jacobean oak staircase and panelling incorporates wonderful carvings, such as serpents on the frieze, and vase-type features on the staircase. When the staircase stops creaking, that is the time we should worry apparently...

On the first landing wall is the 18th century portrait of the handsome ***Richard FitzHerbert.*** On the reverse wall hang three framed documents, all bearing the seal of George III. They are the Ambassador's credentials presented to the heads of state of Spain, France and Russia by Alleyne FitzHerbert, later Lord St. Helens, the younger brother of the first baronet.

Above the oak panelling are two large portraits of ***King George III*** (right), and his Queen Charlotte, by Allan Ramsay, commissioned by the King and given by His Majesty to the first baronet's father. Identical paintings hang in the State Dining Room at Buckingham Palace.

A COPELAND PARIAN BUST 'THE VEILED BRIDE' AFTER RAFAELLE MONTI C.1861

East Drawing Room

Originally 'The Ballroom', we use this room today for private parties and charity functions.

This vignette shows a portrait of one of Tissington's first FitzHerberts, Sir Anthony (1470–1538), Serjeant at Arms to Henry VIII, with one of our four 17th century volumes of the works of Shakespeare.

Dinner service bearing the FitzHerbert arms.

Detail of the room's cornice

Admiral Lord Nelson's celebrated mistress, Lady Hamilton, by renowned late 18th century society portraitist Madame Vigée Le Brun

As with most of the house, it is the panelling which strikes you first. The room was created to feature shoulder-high portraits, such as the four we have here: Nelson's lover, Lady Hamilton by Madame Vigee Le Brun, Lord St. Helens as a young man by Angelica Kauffman, a portrait of his sister Selina FitzHerbert and the picture of Alma Tadema's studio.

The large bay over in the far east section looks out towards the church and parkland. It is a good vantage point from which to see my planting of specimen trees to recreate ancient parkland.

Large Louis XVI marble and ormolu clock surmounted by *'Leda and the Swan'*

THE SILVER FIRE-GRATE
FEATURES TWO
SPECTACULAR CAST RAMS.
IN THE FLICKERING LIGHTS
OF THE FIRE,
THEY REMIND US OF
THE TOMB OF TUTANKHAMUN.

William FitzHerbert by Thomas Hudson, tutor to Joseph Wright of Derby and to Sir Joshua Reynolds.

West Drawing Room

The ***West Drawing Room*** *is different from most of the other rooms in the Hall in that instead of being panelled it is covered in white wallpaper which highlights the pictures beautifully.*

Above the fireplace is a portrait of Selina FitzHerbert holding a vase with roses. The picture of Jonathan, son of Disney Staniforth, with his pet spaniel and a bow and arrow is an especial favourite of mine. There is also an interesting painting of William FitzHerbert by Thomas Hudson from about 1760, showing him with a cricket bat. The oak cabinet is a wonderful piece, with many secret drawers and is fun to show to visitors.

Jonathan Staniforth with his pet spaniel

The hexagonal bay (see above) was added to the West Elevation in 1765 by Joseph Pickford, who designed it as a kind of sun-trap for the ladies to sit in the sunshine and overlook the garden after dinner. Incidentally, the rose gardens below the bay are, for some reason, the most fertile part of the grounds. During World War II a great range of vegetables was grown here as part of the land army effort.

Pulpit Stairs

We now come to the landing of the Pulpit Stairs designed by Mitchell.

Here is a cabinet with some of the family's principal characters in miniature, a marvellous picture of Lord St. Helens and his signet ring and various other items of interest, such as seals. Above hang pictures of various members of the Knight family, a branch of the family tied in with our estates in Warsop, and one of George III by John Singleton Copley.

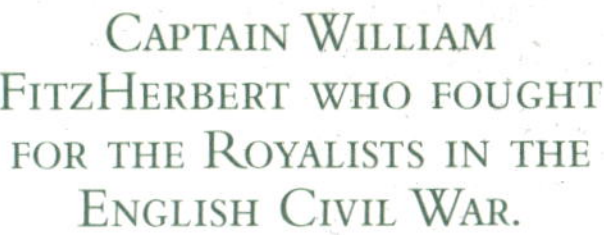

Captain William FitzHerbert who fought for the Royalists in the English Civil War.

Colonel Sir Ralph Knight who fought for the Parliamentarians in the English Civil War.

Sir Henry FitzHerbert (1783–1859), 3rd Baronet, who built most of the cottages standing in the village today.

George III by John Singleton Copley

THE MYSTERIOUS STRANGER
LUKE
CHAPT
24

The Annual Well Dressing Festival is held every Ascension Day (usually in May, depending on Easter) and lasts for one week. Six wells are dressed in the village by means of covering boards coated in damp clay with an intricate montage of flower petals, twigs, coffee beans, moss and spar. Usually the picture will show a scene from the Bible or a line from a well known hymn. Many thousands of people flock to the village for the week and a great deal of money is raised for charity from the proceeds and donations.

HALL WELL

OPPOSITE:
TOWN WELL TISSINGTON

WELL DRESSING

THE WELL DRESSING PROCESSION LEAVING ST. MARY'S CHURCH

The origins of well dressing are not certain but two theories persist: firstly the Black Death plague isolated villages and the healthy inhabitants survived by drinking water from the wells; secondly, in years of great drought, both people and animals alike survived through drinking the water of the wells, which have never been known to dry up.

Tissington Estate

The Estate consists of 2,400 acres comprising 13 farms, 40 cottages and assorted miscellaneous lettings. All the farms have long historical associations with the Estate and are predominantly dairy units interwoven with beef cattle. However the recent problems in the farming industry have necessitated changes in agriculture and I am anxious, wherever possible, to diversify on the Estate.

To that end many of the farms now also provide Bed & Breakfast accommodation. One of the farms has a thriving pony trekking operation and other farms are being encouraged to look at alternative ways of creating income.

Left (from top to bottom):
Well boards soaking in the sun
Village street on an unbusy day
Shaws Farm, Tissington
Village street on a busy day

Above: The Old Vicarage

St. Mary's Church

17th century monument in the chursh to John and Francis FitzHerbert and their wives

My wife and I have successfully facilitated many changes on the Estate including:

- *The opening of the Tissington Nursery for plant sales in the Old Kitchen Gardens*
- *The opening of the Old Coach House Tearooms*
- *The opening of the White Peak Butchery in the Old Slaughterhouse*
- *The opening of the Craft Shop Acanthus in the Old Joiner's Shop*
- *A candle-maker in the Old Forge*
- *The creation of the Tissington Pre-Prep & Kindergarten in the Old School and Old Stable Block*

THE OLD COACH HOUSE provides a full menu of lunches and teas in the award-winning conversion opposite the Church. It is open for parties and functions by appointment and can be easily combined with a visit to the Hall. Tel. 01335 350501

Hall & Garden Opening and Wedding Venue

Tissington Hall & Gardens

(Tel. 01335 352200) are open to the public on 28 advertised days per year. Groups, parties and societies are very welcome by arrangement throughout the year and all enquiries should be addressed to The Estate Office, Tissington, Ashbourne, Derbyshire DE6 IRA.

Wedding Venue

Tissington Hall is registered for weddings and details of our package are available on request from the Estate Office or the website.

The Tissington Pre-Prep & Kindergarten

This thriving school is run by my wife, Caroline. Founded in 1995 with 3 children it now has 90 children on roll with a staff of 12. The school takes children from 2½ to 8 years old and provides a splendid grounding in all aspects of school and social life. The conversion of the 17th century Old Stable Block in 2000 transformed a decaying building into a beautiful schoolhouse with a gym, computer room, art room and three delightful classrooms. It has won many awards for its design and conversion including the CLA Farm Building Award, the CPRE award and a Master Builder Award accolation. Details of the School and a prospectus can be obtained from the School Secretary at The Old Stable Block, Tissington, Ashbourne, Derbyshire DE6 IRA, Tel. 01335 350123.

Lady Caroline with pupils from Tissington Kindergarten